KEYBOARD KINETICS

Techniques for Building Speed and Efficiency on the Keyboard

Written by:
Andrea L. Anaya, BA, CMT

PUBLISHED BY:
CAREER STEP, LLC.
1220 NORTH MAIN STREET, #6
SPRINGVILLE, UT 84663
PHONE: (801) 489-9393
FAX: (801) 491-6645
www.careerstep.com
www.keyboardkinetics.com
#102500

Library of Congress Catalog Card Number: 99-90216
ISBN 1-893418-00-6

Printed in the United States of America

Keyboard Kinetics v.5.5 September 2004

INTRODUCTION

As the world enters the new millennium, computers become more and more integrated into every aspect of both business and personal life. Virtually every career utilizes the computer daily including retail sales, computer programming, graphics and design, education, advertising, teaching, finance, government work, secretarial, medical or legal transcription--the list goes on and on. If you don't already have command of the almighty keyboard, you are being left behind. To keep up in our world community, it is essential to be able to effectively and efficiently navigate the computer.

In addition to the business world, most families now have computers in their homes. Once upon a time, computers were only for high-level "tech-weenies" who not only could master any computer game, but actually understood how the silly things worked. Now, though, they are wonderfully useful for all kinds of tasks, including keeping track of the family budget, balancing the checkbook, doing genealogy, managing photos, or just playing around.

Computers can also connect you to information immediately and from anywhere in the world as you "surf the net." You can keep in touch with your friends and family all over the country and all over the world instantaneously instead of waiting for the postman or paying the cost of a long distance telephone call. These are just a few of the many incredible benefits that a computer can provide.

Whatever your computer task is, a greater command of the keyboard will undoubtedly benefit you. In many careers, a fast typing speed will both increase your employability and make you a more valuable asset to the company by enhancing your productivity. So many jobs require

the use of a computer that proficiency on a keyboard is a valuable and marketable skill.

Even if your job doesn't require typing skills of any kind, as the pace of your life increases, time becomes a commodity of great worth. The faster you are able to type, the more tasks you can accomplish in less time. Instead of penning a long letter to a friend or colleague, you can tap it out quickly on your computer and move on to another task. Students also can cut homework time in half by being able to zip out reports and term papers.

Typing, or keyboarding, is such a valuable skill, both personally and professionally, that all people could benefit from developing or improving it.

This book, strictly speaking, is not a typing tutorial. Most people pick up the basics of hand placement and "how to" in high school or junior high. Even elementary schools are introducing kids to the home row keys and connecting them to the Internet. This book specifically will teach you how to type QUICKLY.

Again, this is not designed to be a comprehensive "how-to-type" tutorial. However, it will provide you with a review of the typing basics just in case it has been a while. If you have never typed before and find that you want more training in the basics, you may wish to purchase an instructional typing book before tackling Keyboard Kinetics.

Because the focus of this book is to increase your typing speed, you will be able to check your progress. After all, you want to make sure you are making progress. There are three typing tests you should take before beginning the speed portion of this book. You will take the same tests again following completion of the exercises. After that, test yourself as often as you wish as you continue to enhance your keyboard skills.

As mentioned, the first part of the book is a typing review. Nobody ever became fast by using the hunt and peck method of typing. Correct finger placement is the first step to increasing your keyboard efficiency. Learn where your hands go and be vigilant about keeping them there.

2

TYPING REVIEW

FINGER PLACEMENT

You should be familiar with the sequence A S D F, J K L ;. This finger setting is considered "home base." These keys are the ones your fingers should rest on when you begin typing and the keys your fingers always come back to. This is what a keyboard looks like:

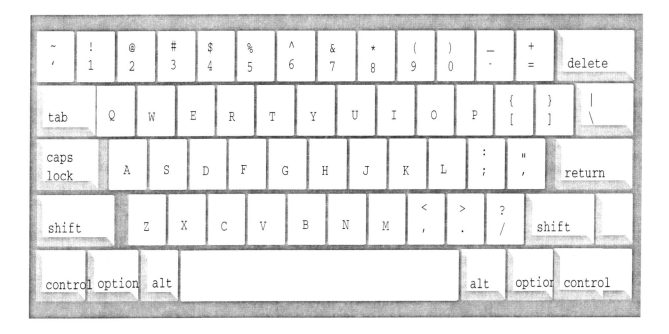

Notice where the home base keys are. When your hands are at rest, your fingers stay on these keys: left little finger on the A and right little finger on the ;. The G and H keys are not "home base" keys. When typing, you move your fingers to the letters above and below the "home base" keys and then immediately put them back. Every key is "assigned" to a certain finger. In order to maximize your efficiency, you need to learn these, and be sure to strike the keys with the appropriate fingers *only*.

LEFT HAND

Left Small Finger

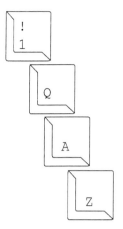

You may notice that this finger has less mobility than the others, making it more difficult to maneuver quickly. With the exception of the A, these are the letters you will be required to type least often.

Left Ring Finger

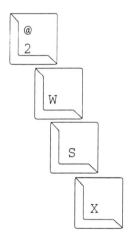

This finger is also somewhat weaker and less mobile than the others. W and X are likewise used less often than the other keys.

Left Middle Finger

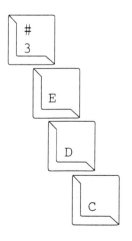

Your middle finger is strong and is therefore used for the letter E (the most commonly used letter in the English language).

4

Left Index Finger

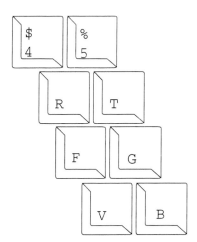

Your index fingers get the best workout. They are responsible for typing the greatest number of letters.

Left Thumb (and Right Thumb)

Both thumbs are responsible for the space bar only.

RIGHT HAND

Right Index Finger

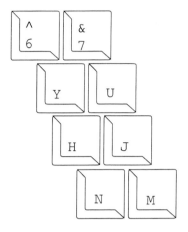

That which is true of the left hand is equally true of the right hand.

Right Middle Finger

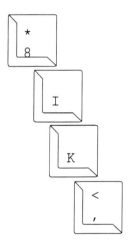

Right Ring Finger

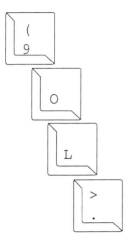

Right Little Finger

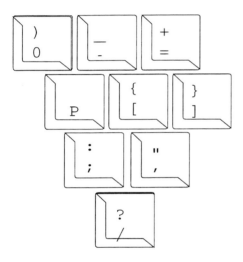

In order to familiarize yourself with the correct finger placement, place the appropriate fingers on the above keys and move them as you would on the keyboard. It is important that you memorize these, not only with your mind, but also with your fingers. It is virtually impossible to accomplish lightning speed as a typist if you have to constantly look at the keyboard.

Memorize the correct finger placement. You should look at your keyboard and know which fingers are supposed to be typing which keys. Your fingers are your greatest asset. They need to be programmed to *automatically* go to whatever letter you are typing. In other words, it

should be an automatic reflex to put your fingers on the right keys. When I haven't typed for awhile, my fingers sometimes "know" how to spell words that my mind doesn't, just because that response is so automated.

NON-LETTER KEYS

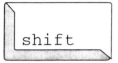 This capitalizes all letters and needs to be pushed simultaneously with the letter. In the case of the number or punctuation keys, it will give you the uppermost symbol shown on the key.

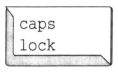 This locks the shift into a permanent position. It gives you the above results without requiring you to push the shift key. It is useful when typing a large amount of capitalized copy. On computers it only capitalizes the letters and not the symbols.

 This moves the "cursor" out a desired number of spaces without requiring the use of the space bar. It is often preprogrammed for every five spaces, but can be set to accommodate your needs.

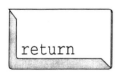 This moves your "cursor" to the beginning of a new line. Most modern typewriters and computer word-processing systems will return automatically. In that event, you will still be required to use this key but only between paragraphs, for formatting, and for other specific keyboard tasks.

This is pressed between every word, *twice after colons and periods.* Your thumbs manipulate this key, and using it will become so automatic you will not even think about it.

8

The best way to learn finger placement so that it is automatic is to practice. Practice is also a significant key to dramatically increasing your speed. The above section can be easily referred to if, at any time, you are uncertain about the proper finger placement for a particular key.

You also may find that you have less dexterity in one finger than another, and it is much easier (and consequently faster) for you to type a particular key with a different finger. For example, I generally hit return with my middle finger of my right hand. Technically speaking, this should be accomplished with your pinky finger. I don't know about other people, but my pinky finger, while it is great at "P" and ";" really throws me off on the return. It is just much more comfortable for me to use my middle finger. In fact, I didn't even notice that I used the "wrong" finger. Somebody was watching me type and pointed it out.

If you find that you have an idiosyncrasy, don't worry about it. Just make sure that it is the exception and not the rule. I cut myself a little slack since I type in excess of 130 net words per minute. I have found that if I try to force an uncomfortable movement, I only slow myself down. So, try to think consistency and speed but don't get overly concerned about something that you may prefer to do differently.

SPEED TYPING

Now that you are comfortable with where things generally are on the keyboard, it is time to master it. Anyone who works on a computer for a living understands the importance of being able to type quickly. The faster you type, the more valuable you are to your employer. With greater typing proficiency, your chances of being hired, even for entry-level positions, dramatically increase, as does your employer's satisfaction with your performance.

In today's world of advanced telecommunications, some jobs allow you to work remotely or on a production basis. This means that you are paid according to the amount of work that you are able to do. Generally, this is calculated on a per-page or per-line basis. Clearly, the more you are able to type in a day, the more $$$ in your pocket. This time is your own, so you want to use it efficiently.

Time is money, regardless of your occupation, even if you utilize your keyboarding skills as a student, a homemaker, or for fun on evenings and weekends. It is undoubtedly in everyone's best interest to master the keyboard, whether increasing your marketable value and income or simply your productive capability and efficiency.

If you are going to improve a skill, you need to chart your progress, and for that you need to be aware of your starting point. There are a few simple rules to keep in mind while you are testing yourself. You should know that you will be able to type faster on a computer than on a typewriter. Furthermore, you can type faster from dictated voice or memory than from copy. (Looking away from your paper or screen will always slow you down.) So, if you are testing

10

yourself on a typewriter, you will be even faster on a computer. If you have a computer at home but use a typewriter at work, you will probably be faster on your home machine.

There are boxes at the end of each of the following typing tests. Write your words per minute score in each of the spaces provided. This will enable you to see exactly how much progress you have made in your typing skills. If you are interested in comparing your speed as you type from copy as opposed to dictation, record a tape of the test or have a friend read it to you and transcribe that. (This is useful for people in careers that require transcribing dictation either from their employers or a recorded voice.)

The following tests are to be taken in one-minute time intervals. Although you should try to go as fast as possible, you should also try to be as accurate as possible. Your efficiency and productivity are as dependent upon your accuracy as upon your raw speed. Your raw speed is called GWPM (gross words per minute) and your speed minus errors is your NWPM (net words per minute). NWPM is calculated by subtracting the total number of errors from the total number of words you type in the one-minute time frame.

One important way you can increase your efficiency as well as your net words per minute, is to concentrate on speed while correcting! Although you should aim for total accuracy when you are typing, nobody is perfect. It is better to correct your mistakes quickly than it is to go back and correct them or wait for a spellchecker to pick them up. I find that I am familiar enough with the keyboard that my fingers can tell I made a mistake even before my eyes can see it. People who have watched me type have been surprised because I am correcting a mistake before they

11

even saw me make it!

Type as much of the following paragraph as you can in a one-minute time period. Try to concentrate on your speed. For this first test, don't try to fix your errors as you go, just get through as much of the paragraph as possible. Determine your words per minute by finding the number closest to where you stopped, adding five if you are directly between two numbers. If you finish the whole paragraph, start over again. (And wow, you are really fast!) In the first box record your total number of words per minute (gross words per minute). In the second box, count your total errors and subtract the number from your gross words per minute, yielding your net words per minute. Good luck.

TEST 1

You are about to embark on a new career that is both
¹⁰

challenging and rewarding. Your ability to type as fast as possible will
²⁰

be an important aspect of your success. A good way to help ensure this
³⁰

success is to make the keyboard your friend. You will spend many long
⁴⁰ ⁵⁰

hours in the future, just you and your keyboard, and for these hours to
⁶⁰

be tolerable they have to be enjoyable. Consider your keyboard an
⁷⁰ ⁸⁰

invaluable tool that requires persistence and patience to master. As a
⁹⁰

vitally important tool of your trade it needs to be treated with respect;
¹⁰⁰ ¹¹⁰

don't make it the recipient of your frustrations. The more at ease you
¹²⁰

are with your keyboard, the more successful you will be.
¹³⁰ ¹³⁷

GWPM

NWPM

Follow the above instructions for the following two tests. Performing three tests will give you a more accurate assessment of your actual speed. Average all three tests for your beginning words per minute. (You get an average by taking the total of all WPM scores and dividing by 3.)

TEST 2

In order to make it through the weeks ahead of dreary [10]

repetition and hard work, think of the sense of accomplishment and [20]

increased confidence that comes with being successful. It is positively [30]

enjoyable to improve yourself and be able to exercise a skill which will [40] [50]

provide you with financial advantages and job security. Typing can be [60]

a tremendous asset in the job market and an asset to you. Typing [70] [80]

mixed with a knowledge of your employer's needs makes you [90]

invaluable. You can use this skill to help in marketing yourself. [100]

Furthermore, your ability to type will increase every time your fingers [120] [130]

hit the keyboard. Eventually it will shock you at how quickly you're [140]

able to recognize a mistake. [150]

60	60
GWPM	**NWPM**

14

TEST 3

Near the center of the state of New York lies an extensive district [10]

of country whose surface is a succession of hills and dales or, to speak [20]

with greater deference to geographical definitions, of mountains and [30] [40]

valleys. It is among these hills that the Delaware takes its rise, and [50]

flowing from the limpid lakes and thousand springs of this region, the [60] [70]

numerous sources of the Susquehanna meander through the valleys, [80]

until, uniting their streams, they form one of the proudest rivers of the [90]

United States. The mountains are generally arable to the tops, although [100] [110]

instances are not great in giving to the country that romantic and [120]

picturesque character which it so eminently possesses. The vales are [130] [140]

narrow with a stream winding through each. [150]

GWPM

NWPM

15

SECTION I

A. Finger exercise. In order to type quickly, you must first train your fingers to <u>move</u> quickly. Practice alternately moving each finger in the air—first slowly, then increasing your speed until you are moving them as fast as you possibly can. This is sort of like a wave, but start with your pinky finger, drop it down while lifting up your ring finger, drop that down as you lift up the middle finger and so on. Keep doing this, and increase the speed each time until all you see is a blur. Alternate doing this exercise on your right hand, then your left several times, and finally both hands together.

Not only does this get your fingers to move more rapidly than they are used to, it also builds up strength. There is very little that we do in our society that requires much finger strength. As a result, most people haven't developed much muscular strength in their fingers. But if your fingers are weak, they will tire easily and you will not be able to type either as quickly or as long. Strength is a great asset in typing agility.

You should perform this exercise often for five to 15 minutes. Do it every day for the first week and then just whenever you think of it after that.

B. Air typing. If it is possible to do so without embarrassing yourself, practice associating the movement of your fingers with their placement on a keyboard, without actually using one. Whenever you are watching television, listening to someone speak, or talking to yourself, "type" in the air the words and sentences you hear. Simply move the appropriate fingers as you would

16

if you were actually typing. This probably sounds ridiculous to you, and you might feel silly doing it. However, it is great practice for being a speedy typist.

Get into the habit of doing this for at least a few weeks or as long as it takes to be able to move the correct finger without having to actually think about it. There are several ways that this exercise is effective in increasing your typing speed. It makes finger association an ingrained response. Anything that is an automatic physical reaction, as opposed to a conscious movement, is faster because it eliminates the step of thinking. Although it doesn't take very long to formulate a single thought, it can really add up when it is required for every click on the keyboard.

Also, it is much easier to type on air than on an actual keyboard. There is no resistance in the air. Consequently, you can move your fingers much faster in the air.

Your fingers are not used to moving as quickly as they are able to. Doing the air typing exercise enables you to increase your basic motor speed—moving your fingers without hesitation and not having to worry about accuracy or hand placement. This enables you to lose your inhibitions about hitting the wrong keys and empowers you with greater confidence. Confidence in your abilities is also extremely important in mastering the keyboard. You should perform this exercise as often as possible.

Finally, this exercise is an effective way to begin associating the spoken word with your keyboard. If you work in a field that requires transcribing dictation, this will benefit you. You will get into the habit of picking up the subtleties of speech and transferring them to the keyboard.

SECTION II

A. First of all, don't stop doing the things you learned in the first section. Until you are pleased with your typing speed, you should continue working on the finger exercises and further reiterating notions of speed and finger association. But, now you are also going to practice moving your fingers as quickly as possible on the actual keyboard.

The exercises in this section will further ingrain associating the correct finger with the correct key. You will begin with your home base keys and work your way through the entire keyboard. As you will be concentrating on only a few letters at a time, try moving your hands just as quickly as you were able to on the first exercise, only this time on the keyboard. The print is large so that you will be able to see clearly and thus read the exercises easily, enabling you to focus all of your attention on your speed. THINK SPEED!! Don't overthink finger placement. Begin by double-checking (by looking) that your hand is in the right place and then just go for it, without worrying about moving your hand or getting it to the right place again.

The following exercises are series of letters, followed by words (wherever possible with the given letter combinations). Type each one as quickly as you possibly can. As you work through these lessons, you will likely find that some are easier for you than others. If this is the case, type the more difficult lessons several times, until you can achieve the same speed no matter what sets of letters you are typing. For example, ASDF should be your fastest, easiest lesson. You don't have to move your fingers up or down, and it is a natural fluid motion which you should have been practicing since the first part of Section I. However, as you move onto

18

the other lessons which begin to incorporate all the letters of the alphabet, as well as numbers and symbols, it will become more difficult because your finger dexterity is not as good.

You may find it interesting that the layout of the keyboard was not designed for optimum speed. The earliest typewriters (which some of you may remember) were manually constructed. There was a bar which went up to the paper when you hit it. If you typed very fast on such a machine, it would easily get jammed. Therefore, it was designed so that some of the most commonly used letters were hit with your least dextrous fingers (the ring and pinky fingers). In subsequent years and with the advent of the computer, they have actually designed a keyboard with maximum speed in mind. Most people (including myself) are reluctant to change, however, and it has never caught on.

Again, when performing the following lessons, concentrate on speed, not on accuracy. Do each lesson several times before you move on--at least do it until you have noticed that your speed has improved.

LESSON 1

ASDFASDFASDFASDFASDFASDFASDFASDFASD

FASDFASDFASDFASDFASDFASDFASDFASDFAS

DFASDFASDFASDFASDFASDFASDFASDFASDFA

ASDFASDFASDFASDFASDFASDFASDFASDFASD

FASDFASDFASDFASDFASDFASDFASDFASDFAS

DADFASDFDFDFADFADFDSADSSDFDFADFDADFSSD

FDSADFADFDFDSADFDFSDSASDDFDSASDFDS

DFDDFADFDDFSDSADFFSADFSSDFASDFDFSDSA

SASDFDSADFFDSDFADAADSDDFFFASDSSDFADAFA

SDFDFDFSADFDSFAFFADSSAFDSAFDSASDFDFSDD

FADS AS AAA DAD DA DA DADS FAS DAFF ADA

ADD ADS FADS SAD DAF FAS ADS FAD SDA FAD

SASS ASDF DAFF FDSA DADS DAA DAA SAD ASA

LESSON 2

JKL;JKL;JKL;JKL;JKL;JKL;JKL;JKL;JKL;JKL;JKL;JK

L;JKL;JKL;JKL;JKL;JKL;JKL;JKL;JKL;JKL;JKL;JKL;J

KL;JKL;JKL;JKL;JKL;JKL;JKL;JKL;JKL;JKL;JKL;JKL

;JKL;JKL;JKL;JKL;JKL;JKL;JKL;JKL;JKL;JKL;JKL;JK

L;JKL;JKL;JKL;JKL;JKL;JKL;JKL;JKL;JKL;JKL;JKL;J

JKL;J;LKJKJL;LKJ;LKJ;LKJ;LKJKJKL;LKJ;LKJJK;LJ;

LKJKL;LKJKJ;LKJKJKL;;;LKJKL;JKJKJL;LKJKJKL;L

KJKJKL;JLKJL;KJKJKL;LKJKJKL;LKJJKL;LKJKJK;L

KJKJ;LKJKJL;LKJ;KJKL;LKJKJ;KLJK;J;KLJKJ;LKJKL

JJKLK;LKKLJKJK;LKJKLLKJ;;LKJL;;KLJ;LJLKJ;LKJ;

LLL KL K;K L;K;L K;LL JLJ JJJ KK JKL; LKJJ JKL JJJ

K;K JKL LLL LJL KKK LKL KLL JJL K;K ;K;L; JLJ

K;K KLK KJK LLL LK J;K J;K;L JJJ JKL L;LL JK; LK

LESSON 3

ASDFASDFASDFASDFASDFASDFASDFASDFASD

JKL;JKL;JKL;JKL;JKL;JKL;JKL;JKL;JKL;JKL;JKL;JK

ASDFASDFASDFASDFASDFASDFASDFASD

JKL;JKL;JKL;JKL;JKL;JKL;JKL;JKL;JKL;JKL;JKL;JK

ASDFJKL;ASDFJKL;ASDFJKL;ASDFJKL;ASDFJKL;AS

ADF;ADKFJ;ALKDFJ;SDKFJA;DLKFJSD;FLKJAD;LLF

JDF;LJASDF;LKJDFLKDJF;LKDJF;LAKJFLKADFFJ;L

ASDFJLKADFJ;DSLKFJLKDJF;LD;JSL;KD;LSADKFJ;

ALDKFJ;ADLFKJD;LKDJF;LD;LKJADF;LKJDADF;LKJ

SDF;LKDJFKDLSD;LDLFKSDJ;FLSKDJASSL;ALSDKF

ADS A LAD KAS FLLK SASS ALASKA KAK DAFF

LAD FAS ADA SAD SAFAD LAKS SKALD JAL KA

KAFKA JA JA KLAD LAD ADS DAFF SKA DAFASS AS

22

LESSON 4

DEDEDEDEDEDEDEDEDEDEDEDEDEDEDEDEDEDE

CDCDCDCDCDCDCDCDCDCDCDCDCDCDCDCDCDC

EDEDEDEDEDEDEDEDEDEDEDEDEDEDEDEDEDED

CDCDCDCDCDCDCDCDCDCDCDCDCDCDCDCDCDC

DDDECECEDECECECDEDCDEDCDECDECDEDCEDD

DADADCDADFDSADFCDADFDCDECADFDEDADDD

AEDFADEDCDEDAFDFSDFECSASDDECDFDSDFCED

CSDSASDCDFDSEDSCDEDSADFSDSDFEDDFSSDFAS

DDESDFSASDFCDASDFDSSDFASDFECDSDADECDS

DCDSDFESDASDCSSDAFEDEEDSEDASEDFDSEASDS

FACE SASS FADS DEAF A FACADE ACED FECES

CASE SAD CAD FADD SEED DEE SAC FACE FADS

CASE EESA SAD DASE CAFF A FACE DEAF SADAS

LESSON 5

KIKIKIKIKIKIKIKIKIKIKIKIKIKIKIKIKIKIKIKIKIKIKIKI

K,K,K,K,K,K,K,K,K,K,K,K,K,K,K,K,K,K,K,K,K,K,K,K,

IKIKIKIKIKIKIKIKIKIKIKIKIKIKIKIKIKIKIKIKIKIKIKIKI

,K,K,K,K,K,K,K,K,K,K,K,K,K,K,K,K,K,K,K,K,K,K,K,K

I,KKI,KI,,KKI,,KIKIK,,KKIK,KKII,KI,KIK,K,II,IK,IK,,

JKIL;LKLIJ;LKJ;LIJ;LK,,;KLJ;I;K,L;KLJJKL;IK,;LKJK

LJIKKJ;KLJLK,KJK;,K;IKJKLLKJ,K;LKJLIK;JLKJIK,K

L;JLIJK;L;L,KIKJ;L;LLKJKJ;KLJKIK,KIL;IKK;L;KJKI,

,KI;LKKIIK;LK;LKLJ;KIK,KJLJLILKJL,KLJLKJLIK,LJ

KIJK,KJL;LIK,LKJLKLIK;LK,IK;KKJI,L;KJLLKJ;LIJK

JIKI LIK KILL I KIK; IKI, L,I,J JILL, K;K;K JIK JLII

K,L,K JKL; JILL LIKK I, JIKI, LJJK KILL ILL I,I K;K

JI KILL KIK KIJ K,K,K LIKK, KJL LIK JIK JJI, LIJI IK

LESSON 6

EDEDEDEDEDEDEDEDEDEDEDEDEDEDEDEDEDEDEDE

IKIKIKIKIKIKIKIKIKIKIKIKIKIKIKIKIKIKIKIK

DCDCDCDCDCDCDCDCDCDCDCDCDCDCDCDCDCDCDCD

K,K,K,K,K,K,K,K,K,K,K,K,K,K,K,K,K,K,K,K,K,K,K

DKCKDKC,DKC,DKC,CKDKEDICKEIDK,CKDIEDEDK

AD;LKCKLDKDKLJLIK,CKEDKC,DKA;LSKSLKDEIIK

;SLDK;SLDKJIKC,DK;LSDKJ;LIDKDKECDKS;LKD;LS

ECDK;ALDK;DLJFFKDL;SDKFJKSL;DECK;ALKDJLIL

KC,DK;EIKCK;LSLKDFJ;LSSLIECK,DKD;L,SDKJDLI

EKC,DKL;DJDCFDLDSDKDLSKEKJ,DICSSLJKDASKI,

DACE JACK I DID CASE LICKED SACK LICE AS I

ALASKA FIJI SIDE SLED CEASED LAKE SAD JILL

SKILL FILL CALD SCALE LEAK SALE LASE SIL IS

LESSON 7

S W S W S W S W S W S W S W S W S W S W S W S W S W S W S W S

S X S X S X S X S X S X S X S X S X S X S X S X S X S X S X S X

W S W S W S W S W S W S W S W S W S W S W S W S W S W S W S W

X S X S X S X S X S X S X S X S X S X S X S X S X S X S X S X S

S W X S W X X S W X S W S X S W S X X S W S X S W S X X S W S W X S

A S D S W S X S D S E D A D F S D S E D S D S F A S W S X S D F A S D S W

S D F A D W S D F A S D S S W S X S D E D A D A S D F S E D D F D E S X C

S D W E S C S D S A D A S D F S W E S D A S D F S D F S W D S W E D S D

A S D F E D S D C S D A D W D F D F S W S D F D S W X S S D F S W X S D

F F W S C F D F A S D S S E W S S D F D S E S D E D W X S F X S F D W S F

SAX CASES SEW FAXES WADE WAX DECA FADES

SAW CASCADE SEED AX FACE FED A SEED DEX

WAS SAW WED WEED WAFED DES SEED FAXES AXE

26

LESSON 8

LOLOLOLOLOLOLOLOLOLOLOLOLOLOLOLOLOLOLOL

.L.L.L.L.L.L.L.L.L.L.L.L.L.L.L.L.L.L.L.L.L.L.L.L.L

OLOLOLOLOLOLOLOLOLOLOLOLOLOLOLOLOLOLOL

.L.L.L.L.L.L.L.L.L.L.L.L.L.L.L.L.L.L.L.L.L.L.L.L.L

OLLL.LOLLLO.LOL.OL.O.LO.LLO.LOL.LO.LL.O.LOL.

LO;LKJ;LKJ;LK;L.LLOL;LKJ;LKJO;LKKJLL.LL;KOLK

JOL;LK.;LKJ;LKJOLLK,JKLIK,;LKJ;IK,;LKKJ;LIK.,.K

;K;LKJ;KLK;OILKJ;LK;LKJ;LKJ;ILK;KL,KLKL;JOLLK

JO;LKJLKIL;KJL,;LK;OL;K;LIKJL;K.,;LKJ;LKJ;LLJO;

IJ;LKOLKJLK;,LKJOLKLKKOL;,KILOKI;LKOJK;LKIL

JOLI LOK; LOOK IK JOOL JILL. JOLK, LOKI L;K;L;

O,O KOOL IJ LIJ OOK LOOK JILK O,O K;K K;L;KO

KOIL LOIJ, JIK; JOIL LOOK OKO LO OOL LOKO O.K.

LESSON 9

SWSWSWSWSWSWSWSWSWSWSWSWSWSWSWS

OLOLOLOLOLOLOLOLOLOLOLOLOLOLOLOL

SXSXSXSXSXSXSXSXSXSXSXSXSXSXSXSX

L.L.L.L.L.L.L.L.L.L.L.L.L.L.L.L.L.L.L.L.L.L.L.L.L.L.L.L.L.L.L

SLWXL.LSOLOSLSLX.SLWOLX.SLXOWLS.XLSLSLX.

SDFL;KJ;LKEDIWOSLXCKSD;LKDKC,S;DLKOWLDK

DFJFKLDL;SASASDLDKWODKC,DLSLWISLDLSOLX

SLA;LDKJFDL;SFKSLWSLLXLSOW;ASLKDFJLX.SLX

LWXL;LSLKDJFASLOLOWLSLASLD;KX.SLDIESLDKJ

FDLDKFJSKLC,LWOPELDLKSLWSKIDSLXLDSALJIO.

JAIL DESKS SOX, LACES KISS SAID I. WAIF WALLS
SEE SAJAK SWALLOW WAIL SAIL LOAD SAD
ALASKA SLEEK DEAF. LOOKED SAW ILL KIDS SOW

LESSON 10

AQAQAQAQAQAQAQAQAQAQAQAQAQAQAQAQAQ

ZAZAZAZAZAZAZAZAZAZAZAZAZAZAZAZAZA

QAQAQAQAQAQAQAQAQAQAQAQAQAQAQAQAQA

AZAZAZAZAZAZAZAZAZAZAZAZAZAZAZAZAZ

QAZAQAZAAQAZAQZAZQAZQAZQAZQAQAQAAZZ

DSAFDSFEEQWQDFCZCADAFDSDAESDFADWADAD

WASDWEAFSDQQESWZSCXACSDZDASXDSEADSEQ

FSDXEAFDSCDAEASZWQSADXCAFDSEWDSFACXD

SESADZCASQESDSGACFZFADSEAWQSADZCADSEQ

SADZCASADSEQSADDAFFDSEDZAFDWAFASQWZAE

ZEE FEEQ DAZED SAFE AZA FEED A SAX WAD SEQ

WAC DAFF ZADDE DAWS SAWED ZEEF AQA SQEEZ

SAD FAD FAZE DEEQE FEED WADED ZED CADDE A

LESSON 11

;P;P;P;P;P;P;P;P;P;P;P;P;P;P;P;P;P;P;P;P;P;P;P;P;P;

/;

P;P;P;P;P;P;P;P;P;P;P;P;P;P;P;P;P;P;P;P;P;P;P;P;P;

/;

P;/;PP;/;;P;//;;P;;/;;P;/;P;/;P;/;/P/;/;/;P/;/P;/P;/P/;P/;/PP;;

JKL;JKJPOL;KJOPI;L.,L;JKKLK;/.;L,KIOL;P;/.LKJJK,

LKIKJKLLOP;;/..,,L;LOIK;LKJLKL;.,LKIOL;PPLOOK;

L,.LKL;;POIL;L;..L,L;//.LKJLK;/.,PP;LOLIIKJ,KLJLK;

J;LOLOL;LK.,;KL;LOIL;K;L;.;PL/LPKJKKLJ;LP;LKJK/

;LLK.LIKOLKLP;L./;LK,KILPL/;PKLJ/;OJLO;PIL;KJL/

POLO KLIPP JOKI PIK PILL JIP LOKI PAJ/ L/K/J/

KIPPI JOLOP PIJ POIL JILL/ LIJ LOOP POOL KIIJ

LILLI. KLIPP JOKI JOLOP LIK/ KIPPI POOL LOP; LIP

LESSON 12

;P;P;P;P;P;P;P;P;P;P;P;P;P;P;P;P;P;P;P;P;P;P;P;P;P

AQAQAQAQAQAQAQAQAQAQAQAQAQAQAQAQ

;/

ZAZAZAZAZAZAZAZAZAZAZAZAZAZAZAZAZ

/ZQA;ZA;Z/PA;/P/;A/P;A/P/AP;PA/PQA;ZAP;AZAQZ;A

ASDLFKJADLFKDFJDLZ;.ZD;KPPQOLDKF;AL.Z;LAK

SDFPAOE;LKDFJDALKFJ;DLKJDLKC;.,;LDKFJSLDKJ

POIEDFKA;LC.,X;LSKDAFKALKSDJL;AKPWASLX.A;

LSA;QPZ;Z;AL;KDS;LSLDL;AS;Z/;ALSDK;JP;S;LKD;

ADKLFJ;LASZZ;LASKL;WLS;LKLS;WKLDS;WSXASL

PLAQ SKALD WALOP SWALLOW KIWI SAP JAZZ,

OW.OW. SLIDE WAQ DOES CLOSE POISE WADE KISS

LOW SAIL JOE WOOED WAILED JAZZED IS LAWS AS

LESSON 13

FRFRFRFRFRFRFRFRFRFRFRFRFRFRFRFRFRF

TFTFTFTFTFTFTFTFTFTFTFTFTFTFTFTFTFT

RFRFRFRFRFRFRFRFRFRFRFRFRFRFRFRFRFR

TFTFTFTFTFTFTFTFTFTFTFTFTFTFTFTFTFT

RFTRFTRFTRFTRFTRFRTFRFTRFTRFTRFTRTRF

ASDFFSTRXCSSRDXCADZFZTRRFDCXSAWAWRERR

TTFDDCXSSAAZXCDDSFFRTTRRESDSADQADZFAA

FXCZDSRETARWESDZCAXSDSFQRQESDZSCZADAD

WERWTWRSFSDAEZCZXADESRWTAFSDXRWEADZC

SFQRSTSFRAEDWCXFADQRSTSDSXSFDATRFSDAD

FAR RATS SECRETS CASE TAR TEAR DEAF EAR

TEST DWARF SAT STEER RACE CARE WAS WET

WERE TAXES SEEDED REACTED RATTED DEAR RAT

LESSON 14

JUJUJUJUJUJUJUJUJUJUJUJUJUJUJUJUJUJUJUJUJU

YJYJYJYJYJYJYJYJYJYJYJYJYJYJYJYJYJYJYJYJYJ

UJUJUJUJUJUJUJUJUJUJUJUJUJUJUJUJUJUJUJUJUJ

YJYJYJYJYJYJYJYJYJYJYJYJYJYJYJYJYJYJYJYJYJ

JUYJUYUJUYUJYUJYUJYUJYUYUJYUUYUJYUYYUY

LKJKLJLKJIUOUYIUOIJ,UOIYUPOJPJPOKP,./;L/KPOI

POIUPIPOK;L/;;P;LKPOIPOK;,,;LKJPUOYPPIJYO,,..;L

POIYJKLIUIOLL./.,;/;LKKOPOILKKIUIYUYUJIKLL,L

KOLPL.,;LPPOOIIUUJKYK,.LKUIIOPL.;LLPOIO;;.,KO

LLKJLKUYKJKJKUYJLKLKJ;KYL;LJLOLJKUYJKYL

YUPPY KIP JULI YIP PILL PUPPY PULL UP ILIK KUK

PIK YUPIK PULLY UP POIJ YUL YOKL LIKKY PIK

JOY JUKO PUK. KOIL;/ YIPPY PULL PULUP YUP PIY

33

LESSON 15

FRFRFRFRFRFRFRFRFRFRFRFRFRFRFRFRFRFRF

JUJUJUJUJUJUJUJUJUJUJUJUJUJUJUJUJUJUJUJ

TFTFTFTFTFTFTFTFTFTFTFTFTFTFTFTFTFTFT

YJYJYJYJYJYJYJYJYJYJYJYJYJYJYJYJYJYJYJ

RUTYJUFJUJYURJURYJUTJFTYJFUTYUJFYRUJYFRY

/;L.JYRTESXSEWERKTDTSWYWWZKLEOP;OIUYYTF

DWQXCSRI.DOLDXSPDSLI.SALO.CSWRO,UYCZQLL.

K;/,KJUYTDSXZAQP;.LKOIUYTREWQA;SXZDCFJK,.

L;POIUYTRFCKJIUYY,.LKCXSDEWFLP;UDXAZOL.,J

UEWSADPOL;./IUJDWSWSS;LDOSYUFLOASFKJLSW

SACRIFICE QUICKLY LEAD PILE PLAQUE YAZOO

WAXY ACID FILL TRIED PRY LATER PARK DECOR

JAIL LIKED, YESTERDAY WAS LIP SWISS LACE YUP

LESSON 16

F G F G F G F G F G F G F G F G F G F G F G F G F G F G F G

F V F V F V F V F V F V F V F V F V F V F V F V F V F V F V

G F G F G F G F G F G F G F G F G F G F G F G F G F G F G F

V F V F V F V F V F V F V F V F V F V F V F V F V F V F V F

V G V G F V G F V G F V G F V F G V F G V F G V F V G F V G F V G

D F E E T A E F A E R A T F G F A D C F S A G T E A E R A T A S D F S D F R

E D F A G E R A Z A S D F A E T E G V A D A G A S D F Q A D F Z F A E R A

S T A D F C V A D F D A S E T Q W E R A S D F A S D F A S D G A S G Z C V

Z C V A S E R Q R S A G V S D C Q D F R G R G F A Z V Z C V A D F A E R Q

T R A T A D F A S D F Z D A F A F F A F V G A V T R A T T A F G F W D Q S D

GETS STAG FAVE SAVE TAXES VAC STRAW VAST

WATER RAD GAS WAG WAS WERE FAD VEX GAT

DAQ VAXX DATE RATE SAC FACT CASE FED AXED

LESSON 17

JHJHJHJHJHJHJHJHJHJHJHJHJHJHJHJHJHJHJHJHJH

NJNJNJNJNJNJNJNJNJNJNJNJNJNJNJNJNJNJNJNJNJ

HJHJHJHJHJHJHJHJHJHJHJHJHJHJHJHJHJHJHJHJHJ

NJNJNJNJNJNJNJNJNJNJNJNJNJNJNJNJNJNNJNJNJN

HNJHJNJHJNHJHJHJJHNJHNJHJNHJHNJNHJJHNJHNJ

KLJ;LIULIKL;JOIUOPIHPOIJNPIHPOIPOIJPNKLL;.;L

KJPOIYUPONPOUYOIHOPNPHIO;LJ;LIUOPILOLNHO

IUYPKL./L;KPOUOIUIYHNNJLK;LK;JOIYIHNUIOKIO

,P.PL.P.;.PL.OK,IJIUHYNUYNHJIJOPKJPKLLLNUHIU

HJJOPKPL,L,KJ;HKJNKJHYUJJLILKH,IUYPKLJPLKJP

JOHN HILL PIN YUP HON ON, IN, UP NIK HIP JOIN

HILL UP H;N;H NILL KOH HOIL LOY PON NIP

JOHNNY PULL PIN HULL IN HIK LONI ON NO PINNY

LESSON 18

FGFGFGFGFGFGFGFGFGFGFGFGFGFGFGFGFG

NJNJNJNJNJNJNJNJNJNJNJNJNJNJNJNJNJNJNJ

VFVFVFVFVFVFVFVFVFVFVFVFVFVFVFVFVF

HJHJHJHJHJHJHJHJHJHJHJHJHJHJHJHJHJHJ

VJFNHJFHGNJFNGHJFNGJFNVJFNHGJFNHGJFNHNH

LKJILNFFPAEITHADFIOAEYAVFDKSJD;;ASDX.SDL

WEIRUFJDLKD,XLSLEORUDKDJVNDJFK,XLKSLZ,A

LQPWOIDKDUELD.XKSLS;SPSLDJKDUWYFHFKDNC

JXHXGSFRWTEUEIEKLDOPELD;.XLS,KAJAUWODLP

SLZOIALDJSIDLCJCNDJVHFDUTTUXLSKAVJXLKJA

DISCOVER   PASADENA   RIGHT   WORD   WEIGHT

DELIVERY CLEANER FOLD ORDER WATCH SERIES

DEV THE LIKE HAIL KING LATE KITE DELVE IL UV

LESSON 19

FBFBFBFBFBFBFBFBFBFBFBFBFBFBFBFBF

MJMJMJMJMJMJMJMJMJMJMJMJMJMJMJMJM

BFBFBFBFBFBFBFBFBFBFBFBFBFBFBFBFB

MJMJMJMJMJMJMJMJMJMJMJMJMJMJMJMJ

FBMJFMBJFMBJFMBJFMBJFBMJFBMJMBJFMFJ

DFLANFPNAPOIERHPOFJLKJ;AFN,EFNLKJFHPIUEY

PIQURADF;ZKNA;KDFHPIEROAHJKVNAVBMNLKJE

RHUIQRBGADFKAERLKJNKMNJKHHHEJAFLKAJF;L

AHFUQWHFKJDNNKLJFHAJKFNEHQPDNZ.HALHQH

FKAJHFKJN,DKNLAKDJHZ,MFHALKOLSQURADNOP

BEST BRING BAROMETER ANATOMY EDITION IN

THE PUMPKIN MICROWAVE CHAIR WALL PEN CUP

BOOK PAPER OTTOMAN GIRL MAN TYPING IS KIN

This sentence contains every letter of the alphabet:

THE QUICK BROWN FOX JUMPS OVER THE LAZY DOG.

THE QUICK BROWN FOX JUMPS OVER THE LAZY DOG.

THE QUICK BROWN FOX JUMPS OVER THE LAZY DOG.

THE QUICK BROWN FOX JUMPS OVER THE LAZY DOG.

THE QUICK BROWN FOX JUMPS OVER THE LAZY DOG.

THE QUICK BROWN FOX JUMPS OVER THE LAZY DOG.

THE QUICK BROWN FOX JUMPS OVER THE LAZY DOG.

THE QUICK BROWN FOX JUMPS OVER THE LAZY DOG.

THE QUICK BROWN FOX JUMPS OVER THE LAZY DOG.

THE QUICK BROWN FOX JUMPS OVER THE LAZY DOG.

THE QUICK BROWN FOX JUMPS OVER THE LAZY DOG.

THE QUICK BROWN FOX JUMPS OVER THE LAZY DOG.

THE QUICK BROWN FOX JUMPS OVER THE LAZY DOG.

THE QUICK BROWN FOX JUMPS OVER THE LAZY DOG.

THE QUICK BROWN FOX JUMPS OVER THE LAZY DOG.

LESSON 20

Q1Q1Q1Q1Q1Q1Q1Q1Q1Q1Q1Q1Q1Q1Q1Q1Q1Q1Q1Q

0P0P0P0P0P0P0P0P0P0P0P0P0P0P0P0P0P0P0P0P0

1Q1Q1Q1Q1Q1Q1Q1Q1Q1Q1Q1Q1Q1Q1Q1Q1Q1Q1Q1

P0P0P0P0P0P0P0P0P0P0P0P0P0P0P0P0P0P0P0P0P

P10PQ10PQ01PQ01PQ01PQ01PQ10PQ01PQ0PQPQQ101

AJPJ10DFOPIL1EOFHJ1KS0WJDOAFARFPIFQWOIKJ

KADFKJPQOJ001OWISKWJ11KLSIW0WKWIGKMDHF

HWI10,DJEOFDPFOIJ1KSDLIJD0K1LKJDSOIP0KLOIJ

LLKJ0,KSPKQK1KSKSIQKSKSDPFOALA;LSOQW1LS

LDLKFAPIF;ZXLKXLL001KSDLSDA;SLPQPLSKDPQD

1 ACE 0 ZERO VALUE OF 1.0 0.1 IS IT THERE BP

100/10 CREATININE 0.1 I AM NUMBER 1. HAVE 0

FEAR A1 0L AQ ;P0 HAS 1 TO GO. COR 0. L.01 TIME

LESSON 21

2W2W2W2W2W2W2W2W2W2W2W2W2W2W2W2W

O9O9O9O9O9O9O9O9O9O9O9O9O9O9O9O9O9O9O

2W2W2W2W2W2W2W2W2W2W2W2W2W2W2W2W

9O9O9O9O9O9O9O9O9O9O9O9O9O9O9O9O9O9O9

W29OW29O2W9O2W92O92O92O292OO292O92O92O29

ADOIW01OIJPEOI029SOCJODJHPEIRHJO1I209SKJIO

RFJLDJEIERJ2SIDS09SLKD0WK2ILKSOI10SL19WKS

K29DKYRYGJVMH10S9XK1KSLKXDJKLSK2KSKDLW

0QKSO99KLSKJSHWK,AKISJH22M,SKQSIQLOSKCJF

APOI1OSDKS0WLKSDO19LK29SLKD019OQP01QSLD

HA2 0.21 THIS DOG BARRETT 90 0.9 WHITE TEETH

O2 REQUIREMENT PO2 209 19 YEAR OLD 91 LB.

TEMPERAMENT 101.9. A OKAY 292 001 100 GO TEAM

LESSON 22

3E3E3E3E3E3E3E3E3E3E3E3E3E3E3E3E3E3E3E3

8I8I8I8I8I8I8I8I8I8I8I8I8I8I8I8I8I8I8I8I8I

E3E3E3E3E3E3E3E3E3E3E3E3E3E3E3E3E3E3E3E

I8I8I8I8I8I8I8I8I8I8I8I8I8I8I8I8I8I8I8I8I8

3I83IE83IE83EI83EI8IE83IE83IE83I8I33EI38EI33I

JFPOIEF09LIJDFOH3OIJOSJO298SLKJFOHVKJAFHPE

92OIJEPOIFWEOP9OIJ2OIJLKJSJZLKAPI1OJSDO090S

DNOQPILJ8JSDIHOLDOI3LKDOFLKJO19189SKSLOW

01KSJDHVNX,SIQOQOIWL1LSODOOSLS9KJDOJ3ISL

1LKSKL02LSDKSO0JIEUOIJOI2O9JSLWO9081SL2013

MAGAZINE 8.3 WEATHER 38.9. QUIET FAST 139/93.

PSA 2.3. 23,000 DOGS UNDER. 32 YEAR OLD. 100

PACK YEAR HX 38.03 HEMOGLOBIN 112/83 BP CBC

LESSON 23

R4R4R4R4R4R4R4R4R4R4R4R4R4R4R4R4R4R

U7U7U7U7U7U7U7U7U7U7U7U7U7U7U7U7U7U7U

4R4R4R4R4R4R4R4R4R4R4R4R4R4R4R4R4R4

7U7U7U7U7U7U7U7U7U7U7U7U7U7U7U7U7U7

4RU47RU47RU47RU74RU74RU74RU74RU4RUR4

DFLIEJOPI7OIJFOIDHJOIJ4OJSODIJ001ILKLCJP01OI

AEPUFOI20SOPFJSDPOFIJPO10WLOSDIOFO02093OL

SJDOFJSD0913POIJSLDJFOJPOI30293874SOJ1OIJSOI

7SDLKFNVNXBAMAUUJ,K,MSHAHXYTWUW92KJDU

YD8WJWH3JHJI2KJJO93893FJJEOPI01987DKSL2932O

WORD HERE 123 DOING IT 4 U. 4 MONTH OLD.

HISTORY CLASS IS GREAT. 140 PACK TEN TEAMS

IN 1987. 23 FEB 91. DATING BACK 24 YRS. 48 LB.

LESSON 24

T5T5T5T5T5T5T5T5T5T5T5T5T5T5T5T5T5T5T5T5T5

Y6Y6Y6Y6Y6Y6Y6Y6Y6Y6Y6Y6Y6Y6Y6Y6Y6Y6Y6Y

5T5T5T5T5T5T5T5T5T5T5T5T5T5T5T5T5T5T5T5T5

6Y6Y6Y6Y6Y6Y6Y6Y6Y6Y6Y6Y6Y6Y6Y6Y6Y6Y6Y6

T6Y56TY5T6Y5T6Y5T6Y5T6Y5T6Y5T65YT65Y5665Y

I2Y5098HFPKNFOIUAYER8072635498FKJNSDVIUHR

9I7YR086350871YIDHFPOSYUTR0987098POJLZKJPOI

UF0I8Y089621847Y12RIHSFOUHAF08761874613IUEH

SDKFUHSOIUY827236481074YKHFO8I7YQIUY198747

2361283HAO9EIUPOP3948709OU10AO1D87390SK203

ALPHABET 21.FOR SCHOOLING. 1986. IN 16 FEB 85.

NUMBERING 123...10. 1.283 BIRTHDAY. RATIO OF

1.9. 56 YEARS. AND STILL LEFT HAND 47 88/53

PRACTICE FAST

You should feel as if you just did an intensive finger workout. By now you should be very comfortable with which finger is responsible to hit which letter on the keyboard. The goal is for you to be ready to move from single letter recognition to sentences and paragraphs. Typing, like most things we do, is a function of the mind. By manipulating the way that your mind processes keyboarding you can also greatly improve your speed.

Regardless of what you are typing, the typed word needs to, on some level, pass through your conscious mind. There are two ways in which this happens—first is to recognize the word which you are typing in your mind and then break it down into its individual letters. Your fingers simultaneously seek out the letters that your mind is rehearsing. For example, the word you are going to type is "discover." Your mind recites the word, letter by letter spelling it out as your fingers type it...

D - I - S - C - O - V - E - R

You are thinking about both how to spell the word and which finger you should use for each individual letter. If you are just beginning to type, or you don't type much, this is likely to be the method you employ 99% of the time. Unfortunately, this is a much slower way to process the information.

The second way in which a word passes through your consciousness and comes out of your fingers is in its entirety, as a single unit. In other words, your mind reads the word, processes how to spell AND type it, and sends it to your fingers without ever breaking it down into its individual letters. You never have to consciously think of how to spell the word. For example, your mind recites the word "the" and your fingers type it, without having to realize that "the" is T - H - E. In your mind, you just think the.

If this sounds unusual or difficult, try typing a simple sentence, such as:

The cat planned to eat fresh mice for dinner.

The most common and simple words in the English language you can probably already type as a unit. Did you notice when you typed the above sentence how your mind processed and passed on "the," "to," and "for"? Did you have to consciously remember how to spell them? Did you at any point consciously think about the individual letters?

Mastering this second scenario for a majority of words is the key to increasing your proficiency. The reason is simple—if your fingers are well trained enough on the keyboard that you never have to THINK about what the letters are and where on the keyboard they are located, you will TYPE FASTER!

The longer you type words, and the more familiar you become with them, you will discover that you can type remarkably increased numbers of them as units. Literally, your fingers

will KNOW how to type them. Therefore, they can type them faster than your conscious mind can spell them. It should be your goal to familiarize your mind and your hands this way with as large of a percentage of words as possible. Simply being aware of this, and making a conscious effort to increase the number of words that you do not need to process, will make it easier to do so. If your work requires frequent repetition of certain words, as in for example, medical or legal transcription, technical writing, business correspondence, etc., consider collecting sources that contain these types of words, and use them for practice, over and over again. You will thereby become familiar with the words you use frequently and can type them at maximum speed, as individual units.

As with anything else, typing requires practice to become perfect. The next several pages of typing are just that—practice. With every word that you type you get one step closer to reaching your desired speed. Keep in mind the things that you have learned throughout the book. Try to type as many words as possible without breaking down the letters, concentrate on speed and not accuracy. Tackle the keyboard with confidence and don't worry about making mistakes. You should know by now where the letters are. You should never have to look at the keyboard. It should be "second nature" to hit the appropriate keys. The words are in large print to make them easier to see at a comfortable distance.

The day passed much as the day before had done. Mrs. Hurst and Miss Bingley had spent some hours of the morning with the invalid, who continued, though slowly, to mend; and in the evening Elizabeth joined their party in the drawing-room. The table, however, did not appear. Mr. Darcy was writing, and Miss Bingley, seated near him, was watching the progress of his letter, and repeatedly calling off his attention by messages to his sister. Mr. Hurst and Mr. Bingley were at piquet, and Mrs. Hurst was observing their game.

Elizabeth took up some needlework and was sufficiently amused in attending to what passed between Darcy and his companion. The perpetual commendations of the lady either on his hand-writing, or on the evenness of his lines, or on the length of his letter, with the perfect unconcern with which her praises were received, formed a curious dialogue, and was exactly in unison with her opinion of each.

To Catherine and Lydia, neither the letter nor its writer were in any degree interesting. It was next to impossible that their cousin should come in a scarlet coat, and it was now some weeks since they had received pleasure from the society of a man in any other color. As for their mother, Mr. Collins' letter had done away much of her ill-will, and she was preparing to see him with a degree of composure, which astonished her husband and daughters.

Mr. Collins was not a sensible man, and the deficiency of nature had been but little assisted by education or society; the greatest part of life having been spent under the guidance of an illiterate and miserly father; and though he belonged to one of the universities, he had merely kept the necessary terms, without forming at it any useful acquaintance. The subjection in which his father had brought him up, had given him originally great humility of manner, but it was now a good deal counteracted by the self-conceit of a weak head, living in retirement, and

the consequential feelings of early and unexpected prosperity. A fortunate chance had recommended him to Lady Catherine de Bourgh when the place was vacant; and the respect which he felt for her high rank, and his veneration for her as his patroness, mingling with a very good opinion of himself, of his authority as a clergyman, and his rights as a rector, made him altogether a mixture of pride and obsequiousness, self-importance and humility.

As no objection was made to the young people's engagement with their aunt, and all Mr. Collins' scruples of leaving Mr. and Mrs. Bennet for a single evening during his visit were most steadily resisted, the coach conveyed him and his five cousins at a suitable hour to Meryton; and the girls had the pleasure of hearing, as they entered the drawing-room, that Mr. Wickham had accepted their uncle's invitation, and was then in the house.

Hope was over, entirely over; and when Jane could attend to the rest

of the letter, she found little, except the professed affection of the writer, that could give her any comfort. Miss Darcy's praise occupied the chief of it. Her many attractions were again dwelt on, and Caroline boasted joyfully of their increasing intimacy, and ventured to predict the accomplishment of the wishes which had been unfolded in her former letter. She wrote also with great pleasure of her brother's being an inmate of Mr. Darcy's house, and mentioned with raptures, some plans of the latter with regard to new furniture.

She could not think of Darcy's leaving Kent, without remembering that his cousin was to go with him; but Colonel Fitzwilliam had made it clear that he had no intentions at all, and agreeable as he was, she did not mean to be unhappy about him.

While settling this point, she was suddenly roused by the sound of the door bell, and her spirits were a little flattered by the idea of its being

Colonel Fitzwilliam himself, who had once before called late in the evening and might now come to enquire particularly after her. But this idea was soon banished, and her spirits were very differently affected, when, to her utter amazement, she saw Mr. Darcy walk into the room. In a hurried manner he immediately began an enquiry after her health, imputing his cold civility. He sat down for a few moments, and then getting up walked about the room. Elizabeth was surprised, but said not a word. After a silence of several minutes he came towards her in an agitated manner.

Our journey here lost the interest arising from beautiful scenery, but we arrived in a few days at Rotterdam, whence we proceeded by sea to England. It was on a clear morning, in the latter days of December, that I first saw the white cliffs of Britain. The banks of the Thames presented a new scene; they were flat but fertile, and almost every town was marked by the remembrance of some story. We saw Tilbury Fort and

remembered the Spanish Armada; Gravesend, Woolsich, and Greenwich - places which I had heard of even in my country.

My affection for my guest increases every day. He excites at once my admiration and my pity to an astonishing degree. How can I see so noble a creature destroyed by misery without feeling the poignant grief? He is so gentle, yet so wise; his mind is so cultivated, and when he speaks, although his words are culled with the choicest art, yet they flow with rapidity and unparalleled eloquence.

He is now much recovered from his illness and is continually on the deck, apparently watching for the sledge that preceded his own. Yet, although unhappy, he is not so utterly occupied by his own misery but that he interests himself deeply in the projects of others. He has frequently conversed with me on mine, which I have communicated to him without disguise. He entered attentively into all my arguments in favor of my eventual success and into every minute detail of the measures

I had taken to savor it. I was easily led by the sympathy which he evinced to use the language of my heart, to give utterance to the burning ardor of my soul, and to say, with all the fervor that warmed me, how gladly I would sacrifice my fortune, my existence, my every hope, to the furtherance of my enterprise. One man's life or death were but a small price to pay for the acquirement of the knowledge which I sought, for the dominion I should acquire and transmit over the elemental foes of our race.

As I spoke, a dark gloom spread over my listener's countenance. At first I perceived that he tried to suppress his emotion; he placed his hands before his eyes, and my voice quivered and failed me as I beheld tears trickle fast from between his fingers; a groan burst from his heaving breast. I paused; at length he spoke, in broken accents: 'Unhappy man! Do you share my madness? Have you drunk also of the intoxication

drought? Hear me; let me reveal my tale, and you will dash the cup from your lips!

It was eight o'clock when we landed; we walked for a short time on the shore, enjoying the transitory light, and then retired to the inn and contemplated the lively scene of waters, woods, and mountains, obscured in darkness, yet still displaying their black outlines.

The wind, which had fallen in the south, now rose with great violence in the west. The moon had reached her summit in the heavens and was beginning to descend; the clouds swept across it swifter than the flight of the vulture and dimmed her rays, while the lake reflected the scene of the busy heavens, rendered still busier by the restless waves that were beginning to rise. Suddenly a heavy storm of rain descended.

I had been calm during the day, but so soon as night obscured the shapes of objects, a thousand fears arose in my mind. I was anxious and watchful, while my right hand grasped a pistol which was hidden in my

55

bosom; every sound terrified me, but I resolved that I would sell my life dearly and not shrink from the conflict until my own life or that of my adversary was extinguished.

Elizabeth observed my agitation for some time in timid and fearful silence, but there was something in my glance which communicated terror to her, and trembling, she asked, 'What is it that agitates you, my dear Victor? What is it you fear?'

'Oh! Peace, peace, my love,' replied I; 'this night, and all will be safe; but this night is dreadful, very dreadful.'

I passed an hour in this state of mind, when suddenly I reflected how fearful the combat which I momentarily expected would be to my wife, and I earnestly entreated her to retire, resolving not to join her until I had obtained some knowledge as to the situation of my enemy.

She left me, and I continued some time walking up and down the passages of the house and inspecting every corner that might afford a

retreat to my adversary. But I discovered no trace of him and was beginning to conjecture that some fortunate chance had intervened to prevent the execution of his menaces when suddenly I heard a shrill and dreadful scream. It came from the room into which Elizabeth had retired. As I heard it, the whole truth rushed into my mind, my arms dropped, the motion of every muscle and fiber was suspended; I could feel the blood trickling in my veins and tingling in my extremities of my limbs. This state lasted but for an instant; the scream was repeated, and I rushed into the room.

While I still hung over her in the agony of despair, I happened to look up. The window of the room had before been darkened, and I felt a kind of panic on seeing the pale yellow of the moon illuminate the chamber. The shutters had been thrown back, and with a sensation of horror not to be described, I saw at the open window a figure the most

hideous and abhorred. A grin was on the face of the monster; he seemed to jeer, as with his fiendish finger he pointed towards the body of my wife. I rushed towards the window, and drawing a pistol from my bosom, fired; but he eluded me, leaped from his station, and running with the swiftness of lightning, plunged into the lake.

The report of the pistol brought a crowd into the room. I pointed to the spot where he had disappeared, and we followed the track with boats; nets were cast, but in vain. After passing several hours, we returned hopeless, most of my companions believing it to have been a form conjured up by my fancy. After having landed, they proceeded to search the country, parties going in different directions among the woods and vines.

The fire from the distant part of the field had driven a single pigeon below the flock to which it belonged, and, frightened with the constant

58

reports of the muskets, it was approaching the spot where the disputants stood, darting first from one side and then to the other, cutting the air with the swiftness of lightning, and making a noise with its wings, not unlike the rushing of a bullet. Unfortunately for the wood chopper, notwithstanding his vaunt, he did not see this bird until it was too late to fire as it approached, and he pulled his trigger at the unlucky moment when it was darting immediately over his head. The bird continued its course with the usual velocity.

Natty lowered the rifle from his arm when the challenge was made, and waiting a moment, until the terrified victim had got in a line with his eye, and had dropped near the bank of the lake, he raised it again with uncommon rapidity, and fired. It might have been chance, or it might have been skill, that produced the result; it was probably a union of both; but the pigeon whirled over in the air, and fell into the lake, with a broken

wing. At the sound of his rifle, both his dogs started from his feet, and in a few minutes they brought out the bird, still alive.

As they pursued their walk in silence, under the row of houses, where the deeper gloom of the evening effectually concealed their persons, no sound reached them, excepting the slow tread of a yoke of oxen, with the rattling of a cart, that were moving along the street in the same direction with themselves. The figure of the teamster was just discernible by the dim light, lounging by the side of his cattle with a listless air, as if fatigued by the toil of the day. At the corner, where the jail stood, the progress of the ladies was impeded, for a moment, by the oxen, who were turned up to the side of the building and given a lock of hay, which they had carried on their necks as a reward for their patient labor. The whole of this was so natural, and so common, that Elizabeth saw nothing to induce a second glance at the team, until she heard the

teamster speaking to his cattle in a low voice:

"Mind yourself, Brindle; will you, sir! Will you!"

The language itself was unusual to oxen, with which all who dwell in a new country are familiar; but there was something in the voice, also, that startled Miss Temple. On turning the corner, she necessarily approached the man, and her look was enabled to detect the person of Oliver Edwards, concealed under the coarse garb of a teamster. Their eyes met at the same instant, and, notwithstanding the gloom and the enveloping cloak of Elizabeth, the recognition was mutual.

The heavy showers that prevailed during the remainder of the day completely stopped the progress of the flames; though glimmering fires were observed during the night, on different parts of the hill, wherever there was a collection of fuel to feed the element. The next day the woods, for many miles, were black and smoking, and were stripped of

every vestige of brush and dead wood; but the pines and hemlocks still reared their heads proudly among the hills, and even the smaller trees of the forest retained a feeble appearance of life and vegetation.

The many tongues of rumor were busy in exaggerating the miraculous escape of Elizabeth; and a report was generally credited that Mohegan had actually perished in the flames. This belief became confirmed, and was indeed rendered probable, when the direful intelligence reached the village that Jotham Riddell, the miner, was found in his hole, nearly dead with suffocation and burnt to such a degree that no hopes were entertained of his life.

The public attention became much alive to the events of the last few days; and just at this crisis, the convicted counterfeiters took them from Natty, and, on the night succeeding the fire, found means to cut through their log prison also, and to escape unpunished. When this news began

to circulate through the village, blended with the fate of Jotham, and the exaggerated and tortured reports of the events on the hill, the popular opinion was freely expressed as to the propriety of seizing such of the fugitives as remained within reach. Men talked of the cave as a secret receptacle of guilt; and as the rumor of ores and metals found its way into the confused medley of conjectures, counterfeiting and everything else that was wicked and dangerous to the peace of society suggested themselves to the busy fancies of the populace.

While the public mind was in this feverish state, it was hinted that the wood had been set on fire by Edwards and the Leatherstocking and that, consequently, they alone were responsible for the damages. This opinion soon gained ground, being most circulated by those who, by their own heedlessness, had caused the evil; and there was one irresistible burst of the common sentiment that an attempt should be made to punish the offenders. Richard was by no means deaf to this appeal, and by noon

he set about in earnest to see the laws executed.

Several stout young men were selected, and taken apart with an appearance of secrecy, where they received some important charge from the Sheriff, immediately under the eyes, but far removed from the ears, of all in the village. Possessed of a knowledge of their duty, these youths hurried into the hills, with a bustling manner, as if the fate of the world depended on their diligence, and, at the same time, with an air of mystery, as great as if they were engaged on secret matters of the state.

At twelve precisely, a drum beat the "long roll" before the "Bole Dragoon," and Richard appeared, accompanied by Captain Hollister, who was clad in his vestments as commander of the "Templeton Light Infantry," when the former demanded of the latter the aid of the posse comitatus, in enforcing the laws of the country. We have not room to record the speeches of the two gentlemen on this occasion, but they are preserved in the columns of the newspaper, which is yet to be found on the file, and are said to be highly creditable to the legal formula of one of

the parties, and to the military precision of the other. Everything had been previously arranged, and as the red-coated drummer continued to roll out his clattering notes, some five-and-twenty privates appeared in the ranks, and arranged themselves in order of battle.

There are, of course, several applications for typing. The following typing exercises are samples of some these. These are only a few. They are provided for you to give you additional practice, as well as to introduce the correct format for word processing applications. If you are unfamiliar with the correct format for a business letter or medical report, you can keep your book on hand and utilize it for reference while typing the following cases:

Business Letter

January 22, 1999

Angela Johnson
ABC Word Processing
123 Anywhere Street
Nowhere, KS 58723

Dear Angela,

Thank you for your inquiry regarding our extensive line of office products.

I hope that you find the information enclosed to be of interest. We do offer bulk discounts, corporate accounts, and can send a representative to introduce you to our full line of products at your convenience.

If you have any questions regarding this information or would like to set up an appointment to meet with a distributor, please contact our office at 800-555-0000.

Sincerely,

Jane Derrek
Sales

Ben Financial Group
12091 Lincoln Ave. Suite 103
Eagle River, AK 99577

July 13, 1999

Ms. Laura Tinel
Technical College
1503 N. University
Benjamin, CO 80213

Dear Ms. Tinel:

The enclosed materials outline the alternative nonfederal student loan and financing programs available through Ben Financial Group. We can help you obtain a variety of alternative loan financial sources that will supplement your existing Title IV programs, or can supply complete funding for your students.

Our goal is to match the needs of your school with the administrative and credit requirements of the loan providers. This is a growing segment of our industry and Ben will continue to work with its school clients to obtain access to the best alternative funding available.

Ben Financial Group provides intensive training and consulting support during the client's startup period. We help you establish an effective loan desk within your school. We assist you in establishing positive working relationships with loan providers.

The programs offered by Ben Financial Group provide a range of alternative funding that can meet the needs of most schools. Loan limits, terms, and credit requirements vary substantially. Most schools are best served by having access to a range of loan programs. We would welcome the opportunity to discuss the programs with you.

Please note that while only two options are presented, there are over ten options that each school can take advantage of, with payouts as high as 100%.

I will contact you again next week to discuss any questions which you may have. Again, thank you for your interest.

Sincerely,

Don Ben

ISBN Agency
R.R. Bowker
121 Chanlon Road
New Providence, NJ   07974

October 19, 1998

To whom it may concern,

Enclosed please find my company application for an ISBN number assignment, along with the Advance Book Information form for one of my books, and required payment.

I received only one blank Advance Book Information form in my packet from you. As you require the entire form with applications, I assumed that I was not authorized to simply make copies of this form. If you require a completed application for each of my books, I will need more forms.

I thank you for your time and attention.

Sincerely,

Ginger Lee
Book Publishing, Inc.

MEDICAL REPORTS

DISCHARGE SUMMARY

DATE OF DISCHARGE: 02-28-96

PRINCIPAL DIAGNOSES FOR ADMISSION
1. Dehydration.
2. Chronic diarrhea.
3. Pancreatic insufficiency.
4. Diabetes mellitus.
5. Homeless.

CHIEF COMPLAINT: Diarrhea, dehydration.

HISTORY OF PRESENT ILLNESS: The patient is a 38-year-old homeless white male with multiple medical problems, including diabetes, who presented to triage the day of admission with multiple complaints of weakness and dehydration. He also complained of a lesion on his left lower leg. This lesion was there for about a month and was draining at times. He had been on p.o. antibiotics. He denied any fever or chills. He complained of a nonproductive cough, no chest pain, and no shortness of breath. He reports that he has been HIV negative within the past six months.

In triage, the patient was found to be orthostatic. He did not complain of any vomiting, but did complain of diffuse abdominal pain and diarrhea. He has recently been taken off insulin secondary to compliance issues with being homeless. He complains of a nine-pound weight loss over the past two years. He denies any night sweats.

PAST MEDICAL HISTORY: (1) Diabetes mellitus. He is currently on glyburide after not being able to tolerate insulin. (2) Hypertension. (3) Gastritis. (4) Status post right great toe fracture, healing satisfactorily.

SOCIAL HISTORY: He is homeless. He is divorced times two. He does have ongoing tobacco and alcohol use; no IV drug use. He denies any unprotected sex. He currently is sleeping in churches.

PHYSICAL EXAMINATION: In triage, the patient was afebrile, pulse 116, blood pressure 94/70 sitting; standing pulse 132, blood pressure 82/58. This is a disheveled white male in no acute distress, able to comply with the examination. Head, eyes, ears, nose, and throat are within normal limits except for poor dentition. Neck: Supple, no lymphadenopathy. Chest: Clear to auscultation. Abdomen:

Soft, no organomegaly, diffusely tender, no rebound. Rectal: No stool in vault. Extremities: Left lower extremity with a 1- to 2-cm lesion with eschar and minimal erythema. Neuro: Intact.

LABORATORY DATA: White count 21, hematocrit 36, platelets 146. Sodium 132, potassium 4.2, BUN 23, creatinine 0.8, glucose 414, ketones negative. Chest x-ray: Negative. EKG: normal sinus rhythm.

HOSPITAL COURSE: The patient was admitted to the medical service and was given aggressive hydration. He was also empirically treated with IV Ancef for 48 hours for his leg wound. However, he remained afebrile and was switched to p.o. Keflex. He was not acidotic and his ketones were negative. He was put on sliding scale insulin. He was given magnesium, thiamine, folate, and multivitamins in his IV fluids. He exhibited no signs of alcohol withdrawal. He was cultured for C. difficile multiple times, all of which were negative. Stool for ova and parasites was negative. However, fecal fat was elevated. He was empirically given a course of Flagyl. CT of the abdomen did reveal a renal cyst. However, this was an incidental finding. Abdominal ultrasound was negative. He was started on Viconase. Small bowel follow-through was negative. GI was consulted and it was felt that his diarrhea was secondary to chronic pancreatic insufficiency. His Viconase was elevated. Please note that he also had a negative PPD during his hospitalization.

DISCHARGE MEDICATIONS
1. Cephadrine 500 mg q.i.d. for 5 days.
2. Flagyl 250 mg one p.o. t.i.d. for 5 days.
3. Trazodone 100 mg q. h.s.
4. Aldactone 25 mg 1 p.o. q. day.
5. Quinapril 10 mg q. day.
6. Viconase eight tablets t.i.d. with meals and 6 at bedtime.
7. Glipizide 10 mg b.i.d.
8. Multivitamins 1 p.o. q.d.
9. Metamucil 1 tsp p.o. q.d.

OPERATIVE REPORT

PRINCIPAL DIAGNOSIS: Left fourth and fifth necrotic toes.

PRINCIPAL PROCEDURE: Left fourth and fifth digit amputation with a digital skin rotation flap.

HISTORY OF PRESENT ILLNESS: The patient is a 77-year-old gentleman who was admitted to the internal medicine service with left fourth and fifth necrotic toes, also with cellulitis of the dorsum of the foot. He was kept on IV antibiotics, his cellulitis improved, and he was taken to the operating room to have his necrotic toes removed.

PROCEDURE: The patient was brought to the operating room and placed in the supine position. All bony prominences were well padded. He underwent a left ankle block after his left lower extremity was prepped and draped in the usual sterile fashion. Esmarch tourniquet was used to just above his ankle. Using a 15 blade, his fourth toe was sharply excised along the base of the necrotic toe. The toe was disarticulated at the fourth metatarsophalangeal joint. A culture of synovial fluid was sent for stat Gram stain and culture. After ellipsing of his fourth toe, attention was turned to the ulcer on the medial half of his fifth toe. This was sharply excised. Then, using sharp dissection, the phalanx of the fifth toe was dissected out, leaving the skin intact. After removing all the bones of his fifth toe, the tourniquet was released. Hemostasis was obtained. The wound was copiously irrigated. After a few loose 2-0 Vicryl sutures were used, the fifth toe rotation flap was trimmed to fit the base of both the fourth and fifth previous digits. Using 3-0 Vicryl, mattress sutures were placed loosely to close the wound. The wound was washed, dried, and dressed in the usual sterile fashion, and the patient was awake and alert. At the end of the case, the patient was sent to the recovery room without any difficulties.

RESUME

HOW TO WRITE A RESUME

OBJECTIVE
Target your objective. "Entry-level position as medical transcriptionist. Goals include gaining experience transcribing medical reports in all medical specialties with emphasis on quality and expedience; expertise with dictation equipment and software packages."

WORK HISTORY
Don't downplay your major achievements. Include measurable results, i.e., increased sales, edited employee handbook, etc. Emphasize skills that would be important to this potential employer.

Answer the following: Did you forge new affiliations or organizations, save your organization money, institute any new system (procedure, program), meet impossible deadlines, coordinate a major project, rescue a project from failure? Did you take on new responsibilities or projects? Did you train anyone? Were you promoted rapidly or rewarded? Did you improve communication in your organization?

Some dynamic verbs to use when describing your activities: Designed, created, engineered, orchestrated, deployed, mobilized, controlled, generated, established, launched, initiated, supervised, directed, targeted, pinpointed, tracked, monitored, managed, coordinated.

Do not mention your reasons for leaving any job. Do not include references or write, "References furnished upon request."

EXAMPLE
Music teacher, 1994 to present. Responsibilities include planning recitals, etc.

Secretary, Student Admissions, Brigham Young University, 1990-1994. Responsibilities included ...organization of ...facilitation of....typing correspondence...etc. "Executed strategic plan that ..."

Secretary, Research Division, Jones Chemical Company, 1987-1990. Responsibilities included...typing technical reports...etc. ("Led the team that...")

EDUCATION
June 1997   Bachelor of Science, University of Utah.
May 1986   Word Perfect, Utah Valley State College.

AWARDS/COMMUNITY SERVICE
Emphasize people-handling skills—ability to build morale, led a team, achieved goal of..., etc.)

The National Association of Female Executives states, "Do not include marital status or number of children. Keep personal data brief and to the point."

Limit to business-related affiliations and committees and activities that demonstrate professional interests or management skills—and describe those skills.

Omit hobbies.

COVER LETTER
"I am enclosing my resume for your review. Please note that..." Here you can emphasize skills or attributes that you feel would qualify you for the job; highlight pertinent portions of your resume. "Please contact me at your earliest convenience for an interview and the opportunity to test with (name of company). Thank you for your consideration."

SCHOOL/COLLEGE

Elizabeth Smith
Social Psychology 350
Section 400
April 8, 1998

Von der Pahlen, B., Ost, B., Lindfors, B., & Lindman, R. (1997). Early antecedents of spouse abuse. Aggressive Behavior, 23, 239-243.

The experimenters in this study were looking for a correlational effect between current aggressive behavior and alcohol consumption and previous exposure to aggressive behavior and paternal alcohol consumption. They hypothesized that paternal drinking would correlate positively with present drinking habits and paternal violence with present aggressiveness and spouse abuse.

There were a total of 38 participants who were involved in this study. There were 19 males taken into police custody for spouse abuse and 19 males taken from a control group (participants recruited from a shopping mall). The mean age was 35 to 37 years, occupations between spouse abusers and members of the control group were linked (unskilled or semiskilled) and the duration of their current marital or cohabitation relationships were matched. All subjects lived in the boundaries of the same police precinct, and informed consent was obtained from both them and their wives. The study was conducted in Finland.

The experimenters conducted structured interviews with the participants in their homes. They determined paternal violence by two questions: "How did your parents get along? and "Describe the atmosphere in your childhood home" (aggressive—3, ordinary—2, secure—1). Paternal drinking was determined from the following two questions: "Describe your father's alcohol use during your

73

childhood" (converted to a monthly intake) and "Was either of your parents an alcoholic?" (Father received a score of 1, mother no score). Finally, present drinking habits were mapped by both frequency and quantity.

All subjects completed the Straus Conflict Tactics Scale which measures family conflict resolution strategies based on reasoning, verbal aggression, and violence.

The results revealed that spouse abusers reported more physical aggression in their present family and recalled more physical aggression in their family of origin than did the controls. Their reported median monthly alcohol intake was significantly higher, and they also recalled significantly more paternal drinking.

The experimenters also created a latent structure model to summarize the risk factors for spouse abuse. Present drinking habits were not linked to present aggressiveness in this model since their association was nonlinear, but paternal drinking and aggressive behaviors were allowed to correlate. This model showed that present heavy drinking habits and, indirectly, paternal drinking were much more important determinants of accumulated violence history (both childhood and present) than were paternal or present aggressiveness. Although present aggressiveness was well predicted by paternal aggressiveness, it was not nearly as closely associated with violence history as were current heavy drinking habits.

The experimenters believe that the small number of subjects and potential validity problems with retrospective data warrant caution with regard to the results of their study. They do believe, however, and state studies supporting it, that recalled experiences regarding drinking and violence are generally reliable. Excessive drinking by their fathers and intra-family violence were recalled

significantly more often by spouse abusers than by control group members. The data leads them to believe that spouse abusers whose behavior closely resembled recalled behavior by their fathers may have learned that physical aggression was admissible in family conflicts when the parties were intoxicated. Regardless of the limits of the study, they believe that excessive drinking is undeniably linked to family violence.

Jonathan Davies
Classical Civilization 241
Section 400

Dynamic Gods
all quotations taken from:
Cook, A., ed. The Odyssey by Homer. New York, 1974.

Civilizations of all kinds and in all eras have relied on deities to improve or explain their existence. The Ancient Greeks are perhaps most well-known for their charismatic, temperamental gods. They believe that the gods influence and affect nearly every aspect of their individual lives. The relationships between the gods and man in The Odyssey exemplify this attitude. The characters consistently recognize the gods' handiwork and implore favors and portents of them. By the same token, the gods involve themselves in the daily activities of the players. This creates a remarkable interdependence between them.

The figures in Book XX of The Odyssey believe in and interact with powerful and personified gods, creating a dynamic relationship between heaven and earth wherein the deities endow gifts, send or deliver signs, and heap misery on mankind.

One component of the relationship between heaven and earth is the blessings or gifts which the gods bestow upon those whom they favor. This can be seen throughout Odysseus' travels in his relationship with the goddess Athene. Book XX begins with Odysseus disturbed beyond sleep by thoughts of the suitors which have imposed upon the hospitality of his family and home. He is consumed with rage and is plotting revenge. When Athene descends from lofty Olympus to confer with Odysseus, she reassures him and before she departs, she "sheds sleep over his eyelids." (line 54) This is a blessing for Odysseus, whom she knows will need his strength and rest in order to meet his objectives and conquer his enemies.

This is just one small example of a gift, in the form of comfort and sleep. Several more can be seen in the story which Penelope imparts to us about the daughters of Pandareus. She calls upon Artemis to relieve her of the burden of mortality and in so doing recounts other times when the gods have intervened with humanity. Specifically, the daughters of Pandareus were orphaned and the gods, or in this case goddesses, took great interest in their well-being and conferred gifts on them. Hera bestowed upon them the gift of wisdom and form. Artemis gave them

stature. Athene taught them how to do "illustrious tasks." (line 72) Finally,

Aphrodite, who had tended to their sustenance earlier, intervened on their behalf to

Father Zeus himself, for good marriages. Clearly, when moved to do so, the gods

are capable of providing mankind with all manner of wondrous gifts.

The gods also send signs of comfort, fortune, or forebodance. To illustrate,

again we can look to Odysseus and his frustrations. As Book XX commences, when

he is stewing over his anger and unhappiness, a sign comes to him in the form of

Athene herself. As a woman, Athene descends from Olympus to give Odysseus a

sign of both comfort and fortune. She tells him that he has nothing to worry about,

for her protection is always upon him. More specifically, she forebodes what will

befall the suitors, by reminding Odysseus that regardless of the odds, he will be

victorious: "if fifty troops of articulate men in ambush were to stand around us,

striving to kill us in war, yet should you drive off their cattle and goodly sheep."

(lines 49-51)

After descending down and promising him thus, Athene departs and

Odysseus sleeps. However, in the morning upon wakening, he openly seeks another

sign, not from Athene but from Father Zeus himself. Odysseus does not ask the gods in vain. Immediately following his appeal, Zeus hears with thundering reply, and then grants Odysseus' request. A mill woman nearby stops working and speaks this sign to her master, "Father Zeus, you who rule over the gods and men, Greatly have you thundered out of the starry heaven, Nor is there a cloud anywhere. You show this as a portent to someone. Fulfill now, even for my poor self, what I say: May the suitors this day for the last and final time partake of a delightful banquet in the halls of Odysseus..." (lines 112-118). Once again, Odysseus is given a symbol by the gods of his impending victory.

Meanwhile, ignorant of his return and their fate, his enemies have ill-begotten plans of their own: to murder Telemachos, Odysseus' son, and take over his home. However, a god-sent portent spurs them to re-examine their plans. In Greece, the use of birds is common in foretelling events and The Odyssey is no exception. As the hated suitors are contriving death, "a bird came to him on the left/A lofty-flying eagle and he held a trembling dove." (lines 242-243) This, again a sign from the gods, causes the murderers to rethink their plan and anxiously implore the gods to

intervene on their behalf by offering all kinds of rich sacrifices hoping to bring their evil cunning to pass.

While the gods do delight in sacrifices from mankind, and often reward them amply, there are other factors which determine who will reap the gods' benevolence. On this particular occasion, it is not the suitors. Instead, Odysseus is the benefactor of the gods' blessings and the suitors are doomed to have heaped upon them misery. Perhaps they are being punished for their imposing upon their host and plotting his destruction. In their cunning they are spurred on by Athene and seal their own doom by offending the home and family of Odysseus. At the dinner (the last that the suitors will ever enjoy), Athene "by no means allowed the bold suitors to refrain from grievous outrage..." (lines 284-285) This results in Ktesippos attempting to harm Odysseus, disguised as the stranger, by throwing an ox's foot at his head. Odysseus agilely avoids the projectile, but the act itself would have resulted immediately in Ktesippos' death by the hands of Telemachos. Not much later, Athene again causes the suitors to affront their host, by arousing "Quenchless laughter in the suitors and set[ting] their wits astray." (line 346)

The suitors are not the only benefactors of malevolence on the part of the gods. In the opening of Book XX, Penelope is plagued by dreams which she perceives as both evil and sent from the gods. "But even the dream that some god sent me were evil." (line 87) The very night that Odysseus sleeps in his own house again, Penelope dreams that he is there. This fills her with "false" hope, because he has not yet revealed himself to her. Therefore, the dream of his presence at her side causes her pain. This pain is, from her standpoint, brought on by the gods.

The gods are capable of bestowing pain and misery on humanity, as well as confounding their designs. Men perceive this, which perpetuates the dynamic relationship between heaven and earth. The Ancient Greeks, as exemplified in The Odyssey interact consciously with their deities. In return they are endowed with all manner of gifts, from sleep and sustenance to stature and advocacy. They receive signs and portents of what is to come, and they are punished for cunning or plagued with misery.

Congratulations! You have completed your first go-through of this material and are probably already able to move your fingers more quickly than you ever thought possible! In fact, they may even be a little sore and tired. Actually, we hope they are. This means that you are exercising them, and as with any other exercise, your fingers will become strengthened. Eventually they will get used to such a strenuous workout and moving so rapidly, and will build up tolerance.

However, if you're serious about increasing your typing speed, you cannot stop now. In the upcoming weeks and months you will need to go through these exercises several times. Each and every time you complete them, you will be closer to typing at the fastest speed possible for you. Make a game of it. Try different things like timing yourself on individual lessons. Using 5 keystrokes as one word, how many words per minute can you type ASDFASDFASDFASDF? Do this using a clock or a stopwatch. You will be surprised at how many you will be able to do— probably even greater than 100! Whatever you do, make it FUN. You are building up a skill that is in high demand all over the country. It's fantastic to have people constantly being impressed by how fast you can type! Whatever you do, do not quit and HAPPY TYPING!

Do not forget that you need to test yourself again using the same tests that you took earlier in this manual. Applying the same instructions, time yourself for one minute and type the

paragraphs on the following pages.

Finally, create your own test. Count the keystrokes in a paragraph of text that is the kind of material you are most likely to type. Mark every ten keystrokes on your selected text, as we have done in this book, and test yourself frequently.

TEST 1

You are about to embark on a new career that is both
[10]

challenging and rewarding. Your ability to type as fast as possible will
[20]

be an important aspect of your success. A good way to help ensure this
[30]

success is to make the keyboard your friend. You will spend many long
[40]   [50]

hours, just you and your keyboard, in the future, and for these hours to
[60]

be tolerable they have to be enjoyable. Consider your keyboard an
[70]   [80]

invaluable tool that requires persistence and patience to master. As a
[90]

vitally important tool of your trade it needs to be treated with respect;
[100]   [110]

don't make it the recipient of your frustrations. The more at ease you
[120]

are with your keyboard, the more successful you will be.
[130]   [137]

GWPM   NWPM

84

TEST 2

10
In order to make it through the weeks ahead of dreary

20
repetition and hard work, think of the sense of accomplishment and

30
increased confidence that comes with being successful. It is positively

40   50
enjoyable to improve yourself and be able to exercise a skill which will

60
provide you with financial advantages and job security. Typing can be

70   80
a tremendous asset in the job market, and an asset to you.   Typing

90
mixed with a knowledge of your employer's needs makes you

100
invaluable. You can use this skill to help in marketing yourself.

120   130
Furthermore, your ability to type will increase every time your fingers

140
hit the keyboard. Eventually it will shock you at how quickly you're

150
able to recognize a mistake.

GWPM   NWPM

TEST 3

Near the center of the State of New York lies an extensive district
of country whose surface is a succession of hills and dales or, to speak
with greater deference to geographical definitions, of mountains and
valleys. It is among these hills that the Delaware takes its rise, and
flowing from the limpid lakes and thousand springs of this region, the
numerous sources of the Susquehanna meander through the valleys,
until, uniting their streams, they form one of the proudest rivers of the
United States. The mountains are generally arable to the tops, although
instances are not great in giving to the country that romantic and
picturesque character which it so eminently possesses. The vales are
narrow with a stream winding through each.

GWPM

NWPM

BIBLIOGRAPHY

Selected quotations taken from the following public access books for your practice.

Austen, Jane. <u>Pride and Prejudice</u>. T. Egerton, 1813.

Cooper, James F. <u>The Pioneers.</u> W.A. Townsend and Company, Riverside Press, 1859.

Use your increased typing speed
*to make **MONEY!***

Have you ever considered a career in
Medical Transcription?

Career Step offers a
complete home study
Medical Transcription
Course which prepares you
for work in or out of the
home. You can train at
home to work at home
using your new typing
skills. The faster you type,
the more money you'll
make doing medical

For more information & a free audio cassette, call 1-800-246-STEP or fill out the form below and mail to:

Career Step, Inc.
1220 N. Main Street, #6
Springville, Utah 84663

Please send me more information about the Career Step Medical Transcription Course

Name _____   Phone _____

Address _____ City _____ Zip _____